AN EXETER MIS-GUIDE

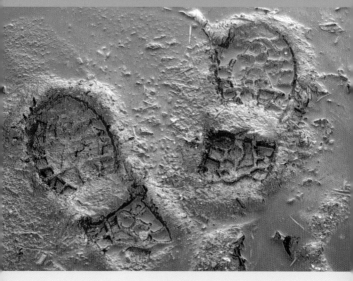

First published 2003.
Words, Photographs and Illustrations copyright
© Stephen Hodge, Simon Persighetti, Phil Smith,
Cathy Turner, Tony Weaver.

Artwork, Design and Art Direction: Tony Weaver.
CAD and Pre-Press: Terry Weaver.

Main text set in Futura: 10pt and 16pt.

www.mis-guide.com

Helpful

Around the city are places - fascinating as spaces -
where you can access more of the memory of the city:
the Devon Records Office and Westcountry Studies
Library (moving soon to Marsh Barton) and the Central
Library with its glorious pre-50 stack - all in Musgrave
Row. The Devon and Exeter Institution in Cathedral
Close. Second hand bookshops. The minds of everyone
around you.

At any point in this book interpret 'walk' as journey,
hop, skip, jump, negotiate on wheels, etc. as
appropriate to your circumstances or mood.

On your journeys it's always worth taking a little
'tool box' of things with you: notebook, camera,
bag for collecting things, torch, chalk...
make up your own.

An Exeter Mis-Guide

Introduction:
Are you misguided?

What's different about this Guide to Exeter? Well, it's not just for tourists, for one thing. Instead it is for everybody to play at being a tourist - or an explorer, an archaeologist, a spy, a fugitive ... you choose. Whatever part you play, this is a mis-guide to seeing and exploring the unfamiliar in Exeter (even in the places you know well).

But even in play the cars hurt you just as much as in the routine, maybe more. So, look left, look right, look deeper.

Walk Bites

Walk Bites appear throughout the Mis-Guide as simple suggestions for journeys of discovery. They do not always relate to the main content of the pages where they appear. They could be regarded as little stumbling blocks that may take you in unexpected directions.

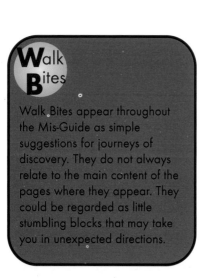

Walk Bites

Where would you place your X on Exeter?

Touch Tours

You may walk down a particular street every day
but only feel it through your shoes. What kinds of
information, sensations, associations arise by touching
the familiar walls and fabric of the city?
It might seem odd to stop to touch-tour your journey
but it can be done momentarily without drawing
attention to your actions. This tour could be taken
on any walk (you can invent your own route) but I
have chosen the High Street because it is such a
public place to encounter this private experience.

Start: Corner of Paris Street/High Street

Railings by the bike stands (Next store)	Touch
Silver birch tree (Virgin Records)	Touch
Flowerbeds (structure and plants)	Touch
Shop windows	Touch
Wooden benches	Touch

Touch

Metal plaque mounted on marble stone (Site of East
Gate)
Carved letters on wooden Exeter Box Office
Stone fascia on H&M shop (Former Barclays Bank)
Black scansions
Flag pole (Bedford Square)
Statue of William Reginald Courtenay (touch his shoes)
Return to High Street crossing it and heading back
towards Boots the Chemist.
Trees
Carole Vincent sculpture of a family group
(it commemorates the Year of the Pedestrian 1988/9 –
How touching!)

Walk Bites Loiter without intent

Where would you go?

The railway, river and canal create borders, edges
which are occupied by those who do not own space.

Between the river and the railway at dawn, we found a
makeshift house.

In the ditch beside the canal path, someone had set
up camp.

In a cave within the bridge walls, a folded blanket and
a tin box.

In a derelict building beside the railway line, the
remnants of a fire.

Sometimes a caravan parks beside the river.

Take a walk along the river, canal or the railway and
look for a place of shelter.

Where would you go tonight, if you had nowhere
to go?

'Fuck-Me' Shoes

Walk **B**ites   Seek and sense invisible boundaries

Black, gold, red, pointed, rounded, strappy... One thing's for certain, the heels are high.

If you don't have any, acquire some.

And walk in them.

Walk through industrial estates. Walk around traffic islands. Walk up hills. Climb fences. Walk through muddy fields. Walk along the tops of walls. Walk along back alleys. Walk through puddles and if there is any, walk through snow and ice. Walk through litter. Walk at dawn, when the streets are occupied by milkmen and street cleaners and the homeless. Walk at dusk along the canal.

Walk until the shoes are ruined.

Walk in the night to the darkest, loneliest, most desolate place you can find. Take off the shoes and leave them there. Walk home barefoot.

Etiquette

When you walk through the crowds on Exeter High Street - in fact when you walk anywhere - your brain doesn't 'see' all the details of buildings or people you pass. The world's too full of complicated things for your brain to deal with them all consciously. What you actually 'see' is an 'optic flow' - the important patterns and details, the crucial information such as 'can I step over that?' Or 'is that too steep?'

Next time you're walking down the High Street use your 'optic flow' to enjoy the patterns of buildings and people eddying and rushing by. Use the flow to greet or swerve, anticipate, nod, smile and veer - enjoy yourself as you finesse the etiquette of walking with, against, towards and across your fellow citizens. And all the time be aware that you are walking the last part of the Icknield Way, come all the way from the coast of East Anglia and about to plunge into the Exe - the once meeting point with the rest of the world - just one more piece of flint on a highway of axes.

When you get to the crossroads of North, South, Fore and High Streets, wait for a break in the traffic, run to the middle of the crossroads, think of water, and then glance up Fore Street to the green hills - and for a moment see an imaginary city covering all the land in view, the ghost of the Manchester that Exeter nearly became. Then get back to safety.

PLAY
SAFELY
IN A
FORBIDDEN
PLACE

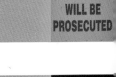

Walking and Stopping

Fill your pocket with loose change. Walk through the centre of town.

Allow yourself to be stopped and diverted as often as possible. Accept these delays for whatever they seem to offer you.

A Saturday afternoon near Christmas is the best time to undertake this walk, offering the maximum number of interruptions.

11.40 Old Tiverton Road:
Road-works force me to cross the street by temporary traffic lights.
11.47 Sidwell Street:
Strong wind blowing hair into my eyes makes me stop to tie it back.
11.48 High Street:
Stop to take a Free Christmas Gift Guide from a stand outside Boots.
11.49 High Street:
Stop to give money to a busker – the old man who plays the accordian. He's playing 'Once in Royal David's City'.
There's a children's fairground ride on the pavement, but I don't have a child with me, so I don't stop.
11.51 High Street:
A man is sitting outside Lloyd's Bank, wearing an old overcoat. I wonder if he's begging. I catch his eye but he doesn't ask me for any money, so I don't stop.
11.52 High Street:
Stop to look at a stall selling nodding dogs.
11.54 Gandy Street:
Stop to give money to a man begging.
11.55 Gandy Street:
Hesitate on seeing a girl sitting outside the sports shop with her head on her knees. Decide she doesn't want to be noticed and walk on.
11.56 Queen Street:
Stop to buy a paper and procure more change.
11.59 Guildhall Shopping Centre:
Pause to read a poster for a carol concert. It's today, at 4.00. The fire fighters' band is playing.
There's another children's fairground ride. But I don't have a child with me.
I stop to read the writing on Gypsy Acora's van. Gypsy Acora has in-born gifts that allow him to read the future. These gifts cannot be learned. His fame is international.
12.05 High Street:
Stop to look at 'magic' Bart Simpson puppets.
12.06 High Street:
Stop to buy a copy of the 'Big Issue'. It's so long since I bought it I hadn't realised the price has gone up. Apologise profusely and pay more. Big Issue Seller wishes me a lovely day, lots of times.
12.10 Princesshay:
Stop to talk to Janis, Polly and friends. They are going down to the Quay to hang out.
12.15 Sidwell Street:
I think I see the man from outside Lloyd's Bank again. He is sitting on the ground next to the alleyway across the street.
He still doesn't seem to be asking anyone for anything.

A to Z of your street.

You may have taken many photographs of events inside the place where you live but do you have any shots of the street where you live?

Make a photo A to Z of the street starting at your own front door.

For example: W = Wall, X = Crossroad, Y = Yellow Lines.

You don't have to be an ace photographer; you can get great results from point-and-click or single-use cameras. Close-up shots of particular features are often more effective than general views. Obviously it is important to honour peoples' privacy to avoid accusations of spying or Paparazzi escapades.

This project can throw up all kinds of issues about private and public spaces. In the process of taking the photographs, neighbours might be rather bemused to see you taking pictures of moss or cracks in the pavement but this should add to the creative adventure. Showing the results to neighbours is likely to arouse interesting conversations about life in your locality. Once the photos have been developed you can make up your own alphabetical guidebook that might include captions, comments or poetry for each image. Offering to show the finished work will allow for a sense of exchange and even lead to further mis-guide projects.

Walk Bites View sky and buildings in puddles

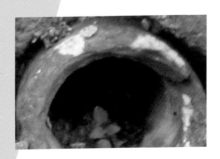

Reverse Archaeology

Look for ruins on which the future can be built. Fallen branches, metal rubbish, waste and dump can all be turned. Make your own statue, make your own thing. Erect a monument to a fictional event.

Imagine new areas of the city, make maps of them.

Make a Bizarre Quarter, a Nostalgic Quarter, a Sinister Quarter, a Cheeky Quarter, whatever Quarter you want ... start with a single existing fragment of a place and build a whole Quarter from it.

Book in for a night with your own John Gavin or Janet Leigh at the 60s Bates Motel annexe of the Devon Hotel at the Old Matford Lane roundabout and map a Horror Quarter of the city in your room (with shower en suite).

Walk Bites

Discover city hedgehog habitats

Crowd Sound Walk (St James' Park)

Check out the football fixtures for Exeter City Football Stadium, St James Park. This is a good Saturday afternoon sound walk. Arrive just after kick-off and skirt around the grounds listening to the murmurs and roars of the crowd. You can adjust the volume by walking through the nearby network of streets.

If you get tired, you can sit on a bench at the unattended St James Railway Station where you can call up train information on a press-button, crackling speaker. The crowd sounds mingle with the occasional passing train. During lulls you may hear the water trickling through the overgrown pump house on the embankment. This is the site of the spring that used to supply water to the city from the 13th to early 20th Centuries via the Underground Passages. The water still flows as an undercurrent to the roar of the contemporary city. If you are nervous of jubilant crowds, leave the neighbourhood before the last whistle.

Time For A Walk 2

Pick any walk in this book.
Try walking it at different times of the day.
Try walking it at different times of the year.
What different qualities are brought to your walking process by varying the time at which you walk?

Time For A Walk 1

Choose a starting point, perhaps the Clock Tower at the end of Queen Street, and go there.

Choose, or use a die to choose, one of the following lengths of time:

1. 1 second
2. 1 minute
3. 1 hour
4. 1 day
5. 1 week
6. 1 year

Drift around Exeter for the chosen period of time.

Repeat with different lengths of time.
What different qualities are brought to your walking process by varying the duration of your walk?

Water Walk 1

For 2 people.
A waterside walk along the River Exe that bisects the city.

Start near Exwick Mills, to the north of the city.
End near Topsham, to the south-east of the city.

This walk has 2 rules:
walk on opposite sides of the river to each other
maintain contact with each other at all times

Possible ways of maintaining contact:
sight
voice
semaphore
flares

Water Walk 2
(for the more ambitious)

As Water Walk 1,

but:
start at the source of the River Exe, on Exmoor in
north Somerset
end at the mouth of the River Exe, at Exmouth and
Dawlish Warren

Futebol

The brains of the Universe
Render themselves reverent
To your genial feet.

Gilka Machado (poem to the Brazilian team)

On a Saturday afternoon during the football season,
St James echoes with the cheers and groans of supporters and
opposition.

As a match is ending, stand outside the ground in St James
Road. During the cholera epidemic, you might have smelled
the smoke of clothes being burned. Do their ashes lie under
the football field? Are they layered over the bones of the poor
buried in 'Mountstephen garden' in the 17th century?

What trace was left by the old travelling menageries? Or the
American troops who trained here in World War II? Imagine
the sounds coming from the pitch belong to either of these.

After the match, drift with the red and white crowd, back
through the town to Central Station... Some years ago, you
might have run into a herd of sheep in York Road, en route
from the goods yard to country farms: a flock meeting a flock.
Turn down Sidwell Street with the rest... Red and white
scarves, red and white shirts and sometimes faces striped with
red and white greasepaint... you're part of a tribe...

A Grecian army, escorted through the city walls by police,
then ushered out again... The club's nickname, 'The Grecians',
predates the team – a term for St Sidwell's Old Boys and
before that, those living in St Sidwell's. Nobody knows for
certain how it evolved:

GREEKS. So we surname, I know not why, the rugged
inhabitants of St Sidwell's. The title seems to have arisen
from their contending with the city at Foot-ball etc., they
being call'd the Greeks as making their invasion and the
Townsmen perhaps Trojans in defending their ground...

Andrew Brice (1737)

Never mind intra-city rivalries, when co-chairman Uri Geller made Darth Vader an honorary director, did City join 'the dark side'?

Let the red and white crowd lead you through a wormhole to Brazil...

1914. Exeter city football team steps off the boat at Rio de Janeiro. A game of football is in progress on the shore. Startled, the chairman, M.J.McGahey notices that the players are 'black as your hat, and most of them playing in bare feet.'

But Rio's best-established clubs were aristocratic and mainly white. Carlos Alberto, the first Mulatto to play for Rio's first team, the Fluminense, whitened his face. When the make-up started to run, the opposition chanted 'Rice Powder! Rice Powder!' and it became the team's nickname. The Fluminense still throw talc in the air before an important match.

(Remember Michael Jackson visiting St James Park?)

The team that played Exeter in 1914 comprised an all-star selection of Rio and São Paulo players:

> The match is considered the debut of the Brazilian national team. About 10,000 spectators saw Brazil win 2-0. Newspapers reported the event as 'simply indescribable'.

> Alex Bellos

Slip back through the wormhole to Exeter, outside McGahey's tobacconist shop on the High Street.

Turn off into a side street. Leave the crowd.

Uri Geller, the team's co-chairman, hoped to persuade Brazil to a return match in 2002.

They declined.

 Find red Exeter, amber Exeter, green Exeter

Debenhams Cathedral Views

Ascend by lift to the 5th Floor of the Debenhams
Department Store on the corner of Sidwell Street and
New North Road. Go to the Restaurant where you will
find a special platform for viewing the city.
Place the buildings onto the surrounding hills.
Leave the Cathedral where it is.
Place the colours and textures of the hills into this new
blank arena.
Follow the flight of a passing bird.
Where it lands or disappears could indicate the
direction for your next walk.
Focus upon someone walking in the High Street below.
Keep him/her in view for as long as possible.

After the third bus passes, go and order a cup of tea.
Sit down and remember the birds'-eye views you have
had during your lifetime.
After tea, take one more look out of the window
and then take the lift to street level.
Exit from the store and cross New North Road at the
pedestrian crossing.
Once across, look up at Debenhams and identify the
window named Cathedral View.

Now walk in the direction where the bird landed.

Walk For Exhibitionists or Reality-TV-show Wannabes

A walk along the High Street, connecting the green municipal CCTV towers.

Start outside Next.
End at the junction with South Street.

As you walk keep your eyes peeled for as many cameras as possible.

Potential tactics:
put on your best clothes and make-up
show off as much as possible
'make love' to the cameras
create routines to perform to anonymous viewers
knock up placards with messages on them and parade them in front of the cameras

Rural Relic, Urban Reliquary

Look for the city in the country and the country in the city. There are swathes of disorganised greenery throughout Exeter - old rural lanes and paths, even near the centre of the city. Every time we drift through the urban streets we swiftly find ourselves hitting the countryside.

But then, once in the country, we stumble over rules and regulations and piles of litter. The land always belongs to someone, is caught in the web of commerce and communication. If this is 'the country', it is not 'the wild'. The green world and the city are not separate, but intricately connected, each to be found within the other.

Go to the edges of the city, where city and country meet. Take a Polaroid camera and take pictures of what you find. Write the time and a fragment of text on them. This can relate to anything around you.

Walk in, towards the centre. Place the pictures somewhere along your route.

In March 2001, we walked from the motorway service station, along Apple Lane, then Apple Lane Path before turning right, down past Sowton and Digby Station and back into town along Quarry Lane. During the first half of our route, we aimed to take polaroids of the country, but soon found we were photographing an odd mix of city and country merging. As we continued through Heavitree, we posted our polaroids along the route. Puzzling little relics of the city's outskirts, left for other people to find.

Many Ways on Many Ways

There are many ways of travelling the city. In many guises, many skins. Sometimes we see the big differences, miss the small ones. A few moments chatting about the shapes and surfaces of the city with members of Shopmobility - an organisation helping to provide transport solutions for less mobile people in and round Exeter, people who see the city from closer to the ground than most adults - and you'll begin to be aware of small stone lips everywhere, subtle changes of gradient, the borders of one texture and another, angles and grips.

You may come to distrust tarmac; its shiny smoothness on a sunny day hiding a shuddering ripple. To be surprised by the sympathy of larger cobbles to wheels. To enjoy the eruptions and juxtapositions of granite kerbstones with equanimity; but to then back your judgement of exact angles and grip against a tipping wheelchair throwing you into the middle of traffic. Looking closer you see the beauty and the danger are together.

These marks, boundaries, lumps and slopes on the city's surface are psychosomatic signs of razing, uprooting and re-laying. One example: like the church names the patterns at the very heart of the city bear witness to the borders of a former British minority community living 'at peace, but without mixture; like oil and water in a glass' with a Saxon majority, until ethnically cleansed by 'Saint' Athelstan and Edward the Confessor - 'Little Brittain' (around the present Picture House) testimony to a pre-Christian culture, ghettoised and then 'expelled'. No surprise then that disruptions like that show up in the pavements; shaking down the centuries and tapping at the spines of wheelchair and scooter users.

Even with more drop kerbs around there are few long pleasurable runs for wheels in an Exeter of choppings and changings with its swirling currents of shoppers, workers, visitors, children, skateboarders, explorers and street entertainers. The new paving at the High Street end of Queen Street is a joy jolted from its seat by the rich and imperious flags outside the Museum, great pages of stone read quite differently by their various traversers, if it hasn't already been slid from underneath itself on metal tactiles on a wet day - (tactiles: raised bubbles in the pavement placed at crossing points for the benefit of visually impaired travellers).

Shopmobility are open to sharing their understandings of the city; if you're able-bodied and seriously interested in discovering how the city feels from a different per-spective then Shopmobility can make one of their vehicles available when not in use by regular users: ring them on 01392 494001.

Walk Bites Identify buggy routes for trundling baby to sleep

Paved Paradise

Although Paris Street, home of the Civic Centre (complete with nuclear bunker), was built to replace a road called 'Shitbrook Street', its newer name has prettier connotations – though not of France's capital.

According to Hazel Harvey, 'Paris' might come from the French word 'Pareis', or the Latin, 'Paradisus', meaning 'enclosure'. She cites a record that credits Paris Street with 'a garden called Paradys'.

Find the place where
you think the garden
might have been, or
where lovers might
tryst nowadays.
Place a red rose to
mark the spot (the
rent for this garden in
the 13th Century).

Dread places

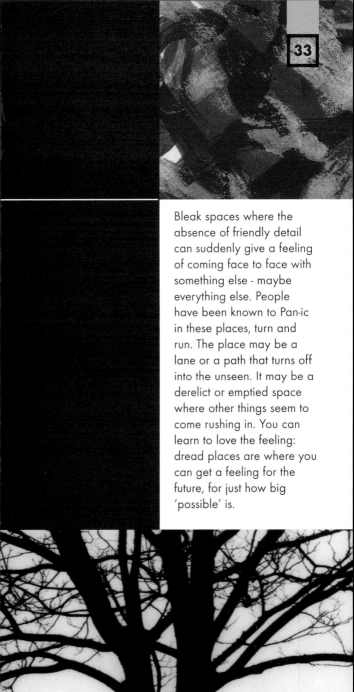

Bleak spaces where the absence of friendly detail can suddenly give a feeling of coming face to face with something else - maybe everything else. People have been known to Pan-ic in these places, turn and run. The place may be a lane or a path that turns off into the unseen. It may be a derelict or emptied space where other things seem to come rushing in. You can learn to love the feeling: dread places are where you can get a feeling for the future, for just how big 'possible' is.

Drifting Exeter

To get to the strange and magical places of Exeter you need a kind of walking that disrupts your usual getting about like going shopping, or to work or school, to the movies, moseying around tourist spots or attending church, synagogue or mosque. Or bingo. Drifting means disrupting all those things - even the flow of family life.

A few tips for disrupting your routine:

Start at an unusual time - very early in the morning, or in the middle of a working day, or late at night.

Start at an unusual place - you can use a 'catapult' - for example, if you're feeling flush you could call a cab, hand over a couple of notes, strap on walkmans and blindfolds and ask the driver to drop you off somewhere without recognisable landmarks. Or you can leap on buses without knowing their destinations.

Once you are walking, don't follow a map. Follow your feelings. Follow shapes. Or, say, take the first left turning, then the next right, then the next left and so on... avoid buying things, go against the flow.

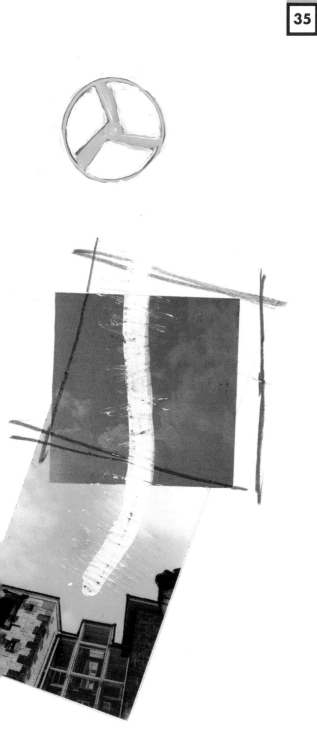

Nostalgic Drift (for those who know the City well)

Revisit scenes from your past and see how they're getting along without you. Look into the back gardens of houses you used to inhabit. Commemorate in chalk special places on the pavement where you said 'Goodbye' or had a memorable conversation, or kissed. Lay a wreath on the site of a memory you want to put to rest.

Compass Walk 1

Get a compass.

Choose:
a starting point, perhaps somewhere in West Avenue
a compass course
a length of time to walk for

Walk for the chosen period of time in the chosen direction.

Do your utmost not to deviate from your straight course.

To walk a line is the easiest thing a human being can do to put his [her] mark on a place.

Richard Long

Compass Walk 2

Get a pair of compasses, a ruler and a map of Exeter.

Choose:
a starting point, perhaps outside 82 Longbrook Street, the childhood home of the mathematician, William Kingdon Clifford
a distance that you wish to walk

Dredge up the residual knowledge from your school maths lessons.

Divide the distance that you wish to walk by 6 (approximately 2π).
Consult the map's scale and use the ruler to set the pair of compasses to required radius.

For example:
you wish to do a 3 kilometre walk and your map is 1:25000
divide 3km by 6 to get 0.5km
on a 1:25000 map 1km is represented by 2.5cm
therefore 0.5km is represented by 1.25cm
so set your pair of compasses to this distance

Use the pair of compasses to draw a circle on your map, making sure that your starting point is on the circumference.

Walk the circumference.

Do your utmost not to deviate from your circular course.

'sploring

Go drifting with a child or children. Let the children choose your direction at each junction. Call it 'exploring'. Maybe take a notebook for them to write their thoughts in or for you to record for them.

Dog-leg

Borrow a dog from a friend.

Let it take you for a walk.

@Virtual Displacement

```
To: g.venus@wiz.co.uk

>Dear Geraldine, I herewith
send you the stone angels of
Exeter Cathedral.
>They are floodlit with an
orange glow. Hope you enjoy
them,
>Love from Simon XXXXX
```

There are probably many things you love about Exeter but are there particular places that you loath?
For example, is there a factory that pumps out revolting smells or a building with noisy air conditioning fans that keep you awake at night?
Why not use e.mail to transport such places somewhere else?

The smelly factory could be sent to the e.mail address of a famous perfume manufacturers; the noisy building could be dispatched to a music festival where the sound would be drowned out by Drum'n'Bass. This mis-guide act may not effect any discernible change but the virtual displacement might make you feel better.
An alternative version of this e.mail project could be to send a place you love to someone you love.

If you do not have access to home e.mail you could use the local library facilities or a cyber café.

Sightsee a supermarket but do not buy anything

To: chanel@scent.org.uk

>Dear Chanel Number 4, It is with some optimism that I herewith present you
>HENRY SWILES LTD, HOOF GLUE MANUFACTURERS, EXETER.
>Hope you can do something about the aroma. Good Luck, Simon.

Told Off

'Watch Out For That Child With Boiling Water' – sign, warning of a psychopathic youngster on the loose, Debenhams Restaurant, fifth floor.

Find the succour and salvation awaiting you at the Toc H Hall. The sign on the side of Rose Cottage, 32 Whipton Village Road, behind Whipton shops, points the way. Spend eternity searching if you have to.

To enjoy being soaked with signs try Tilly's Tea Parlour on Sidwell Street for a full immersion. Leave your own sign there on a slip of paper.

Outside, replenished, read the signs on the city's surfaces: drips of blood after the weekend, the vomit of the university terms, smashed animals pressed like flowers in the city's outer layers – a repartee between machines and 'the others'.

Extremes

Within Exeter, walk from:

the most southerly place to the most northerly place
the lowest place to the highest place
the oldest place to the newest place
the ugliest place to the most beautiful place
the most natural place to the most synthetic place
the busiest place to the stillest place
the most provincial place to the most metropolitan place
the saddest place to the happiest place
the most intelligent place to the most stupid place
the bravest place to the most cowardly place
the most impotent place to the most sexually-charged place
etc.

One Way

Visit the following sets of roads:
George Street, Market Street, Smythen Street, King Street & Preston Street
Colleton Crescent, Melbourne Place, Friars Walk & Lucky Lane
Southernhay East, Southernhay West, Post Office Street & Bluecoat Lane

The road signs will tell you that there is only 'one way' to navigate each area.

Find other ways of mapping and signing routes through these public spaces.

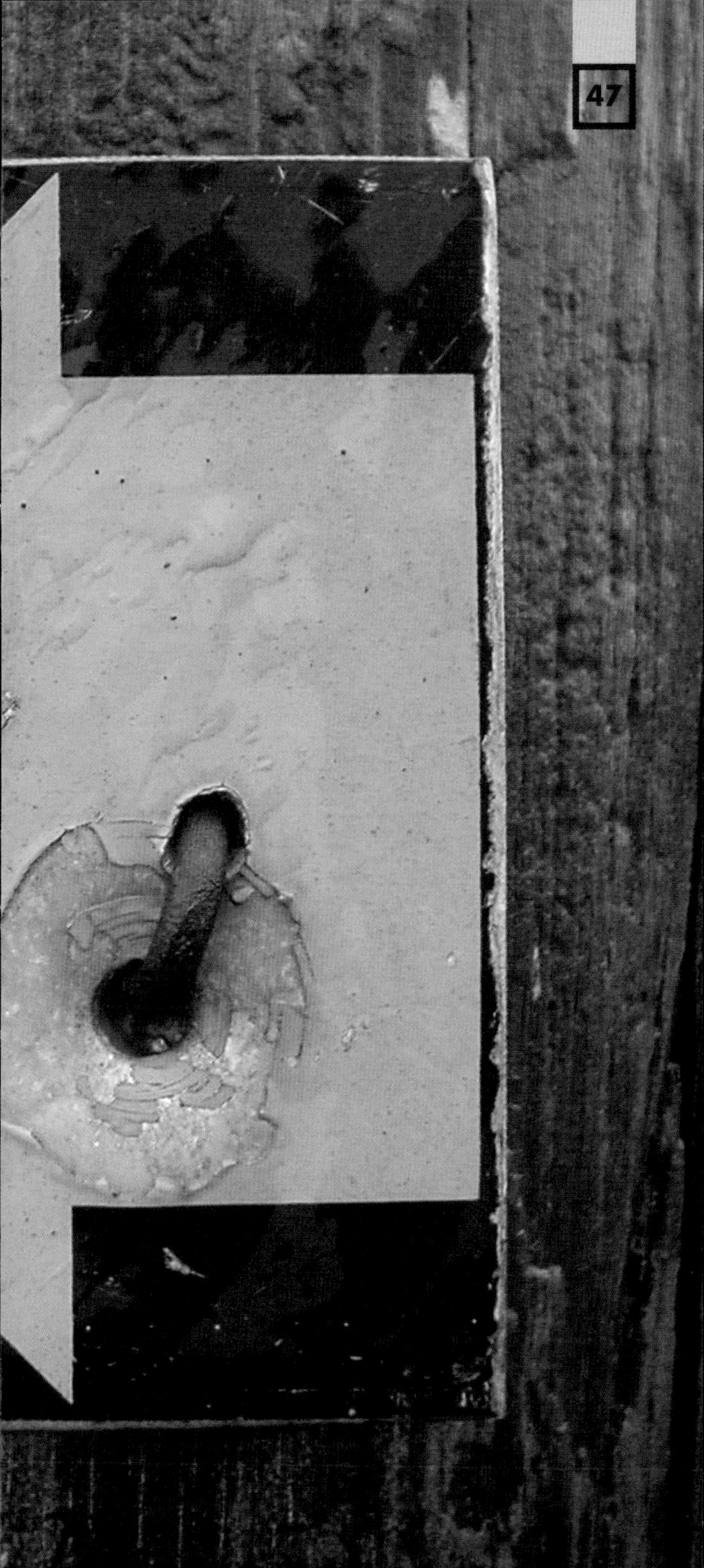

The Space Between

Go out of your house and look at your road. How many road signs does it have? How many lines are painted on the road? Have you noticed them before?

(It was not until I saw a surveyor's photograph of the house we were trying to buy, that I saw it had a 'dead end' sign placed prominently in front of it. I hoped it was not an omen.)

Walk in any direction, observing street signs, markings, bollards, textured pavement and coloured tarmac. Try to imagine the space without them being there.

Streets in cities serve many purposes [...] if a city's streets look interesting, the city looks interesting.

Jane Jacobs

Attempt to obey these signs as a pedestrian. You may have to invent actions for some signs. Where a sign appears repeatedly (for example, on a roundabout) repeat the action once for each sign.

Count the number of painted bicycles and people.

As you walk, look out for the shortest section of green cycle path in the city.

Planning permissions are granted or withheld under the Planning Acts (1947). No such system controls the space between the buildings.

Count the uprights at the crossroads by Pinhoe
Sainsbury's.

Notice the signs attached to the city wall.

Who is the street for? Motorists, cyclists or pedestrians?

Finally, (on another occasion if need be), visit Castle
Street and Castle Square, in front of the Courts, and
observe the new layout.

Simplicity [...] is always, always the answer.

Malcolm Haste

Peace Walk

In 1953, a woman known only as 'Peace Pilgrim' began a journey which she vowed would continue until the world learned the ways of peace. She walked over 25,000 miles through the United States of America. This was not the first or the last time that anyone walked for peace, though she probably walked the furthest.

Go on a pilgrimage for peace, linking the Synagogue (Synagogue Place, Mary Arches) to the Cathedral and then on to the Mosque (York Road). Or you might join up the Jewish graveyard (Magdalen Street) with St. David's Church (St. David's Hill) and the Centre for Arabic and Islamic Studies on Streatham Campus. Or create your own pilgrimage.

The Buddha walked for inner peace. He said, 'Peace in the world and peace in our hearts are deeply connected.' Mahavir, the founder of the Jain religion, was enlightened while walking. Mahatma Gandhi walked to the sea and made salt as a non-violent action for the freedom of India. Martin Luther King organised a great walk to Washington to end racialism.

Satish Kumar

Sex walk

From the Loveshack, a suitably mechanical setting among car part shops in Verney Street, via Ann Summers in the High Street - detour down South Street, around Kalenderhay Lane, back across South Street and down Guinea Street - all sites of historic and absent brothels on the cusp between the West Quarter and respectability, past the long-gone shade of the notorious Pestle & Mortar (any rude symbolism there?), then right down Market Street, left and cross over Fore Street to the Private Shop sex shop... then right up Bartholomew Street, cutting right when you can into what's between North Street and Mary Arches Street for more old brothel sites... then you can change the whole kind of sex and walk back down Fore Street, this time checking out the pubs and clubs, alive and packed for weekend courtship rituals. Then take the side streets and imagine 'scenes' that you know nothing of... invent inclinations and desires and secretly fit them to spaces, places, addresses (and they are probably there), then wander further and find sensual buildings and erotic landscapes, distant hills like velvet clinging to... cruise a little... pick someone up...

The Memory of Water

This walk roughly follows the course of a stream that used to flow above ground: The Long Brook. Look for the memory of water along the route; play the detective in working out where the brook used to flow.

Start at the willow tree in Willow Walk, where the steam laundry used to be. Walk down the former farm drive, through 'Lion's Holt' to Well Street.

At the railway bridge, turn right and go down to the platform. Look for water.

Turn back and cross the bridge. Take the steps down to the opposite platform. Look for a well. Turn back and walk on up Well Street.

Keep looking for water, or images of water, or traces of water.

At the end of the road, turn right past St. Sidwell's School, opposite the site of St. Sidwell's Well. Christian saint or fertility symbol? A girl or a spring or a sheaf of corn?

Walk down Queen's Crescent to Longbrook Street. Read the inscription above the door to Harry's Restaurant. Look for traces of the brook's course.

Walk along Longbrook Terrace to New North Road. Cross the road and take the 'Bird Cage' path along the side of Central Station, trying to imagine swimmers underneath willow trees.

At Queen Street, cross the road and go down Northernhay Street to the Iron Bridge. At the bottom, walk under the bridge and look back. Where did the brook flow?

Walk along Exe Street. The Long Brook ran along here. On Bonhay Road, turn left (without crossing) and walk over the grass verge to find water. Follow it as far as it goes.

Botanising on the asphalt

Exeter University Campus is said to be home to a range of plants second only to Kew. Just outside Exeter, Veitch's gardens at Killerton are particularly beautiful when the magnolias are in flower.

But why not look for plants in unexpected places as well? Look for wild flowers growing in industrial estates, building sites, road verges, or between the paving stones. Take a guidebook to identify them, or just enjoy their patches of colour.

Behind the hoardings opposite the motorway service station is a piece of wasteland covered in wildflowers. Further into Sowton industrial estate, I found a grass patch with lakes of speedwell. Buttercups and daisies grow across desire paths. Bluebells forget the day they were planted and spread themselves in front of warehouses.

Plants have their own geographies. Many of the flowers are immigrants, some of them escaping from garden boundaries. Others were once grown as animal feed or medicines but have made themselves common everywhere.

Germander speedwell - farewell, goodbye - came from South-West Asia and is here to stay. Sewn into a traveller's coat it's said to bring luck. Ivy-leaved toadflax, found in walls all over Exeter, may have arrived in marble statues brought from Italy to Oxford. Golden melilot could have been introduced by sixteenth century herbalists. White campion is supposed to have arrived in the Stone Age from Southern Europe. Red valerian, or 'drunkards', brought in by Mediterranean sailors, staggered out of gardens to hang out by the roadside, especially in the South West. Buddleia was found in the mountains on the border between China and Tibet by French Missionaries who brought it to

Europe. It's developed a taste for travel and grows along railway lines, its seeds spreading along their corridors, whirled along in the slipstreams of trains.

If you prefer a greater density of wild flowers, why not take a walk through Mincinglake Park where in May there are bluebells, whitebells, vetches and where oxe eye daisies are scattered like huge flakes of snow across the grass?

 Walk Bites Skip over Trews Weir bouncy bridge

Looking Skywards

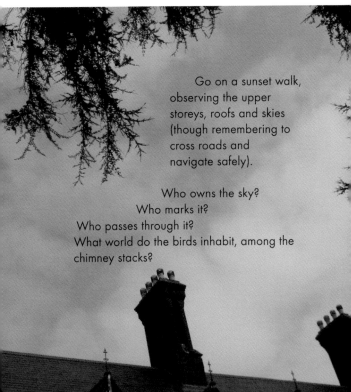

Go on a sunset walk, observing the upper storeys, roofs and skies (though remembering to cross roads and navigate safely).

Who owns the sky?
Who marks it?
Who passes through it?
What world do the birds inhabit, among the chimney stacks?

Urban safari

Dinosaurs in the café, rearing horses, contending bulls and griffon on the Clock Tower, eagles on the insurance building, the memorial to two dogs - Charity and Racism - the ghost of a wood bear that once clutched a pint there, winged horses, the dragon trodden by Victory - track up the steps of the Royal Albert Memorial Museum to the Natural History Room - a museum of a museum, a way of seeing has been stuffed and stretched so we can see it - that elephant destroyed part of one wall to get in, the skull of the river crocodile is unlikely to be matched in the wild again, the bison on its bathroom carpet? Latest mutation of a collection of collections, partly the shootings of C. V. A. Peel. How fictional is his 1927 novel 'The Ideal Island'? 'What a relief it would be to get away from the hateful existence one spends in dirty cities!' A thinly disguised Peel sets off with 11 men and 12 women, two Maxim guns and 'a limited number of cigars for the men' to make Utopia on an island in the Southern Hemisphere. They commit genocide, are 'betrayed' by 'the Engineer' and driven off by volcanic Nature. Now Peel's collection is housed in a building clad in lava. Outside again... track the weathervane, part cockerel part dragon, remnant of the old North Gate - on a building beside the Ironbridge was a stone bird, marking what had once been the Falcon Inn. Now building and stone have gone the bird is free from the spell of the White Witch to fly around the spire of Hermes' temple, a peregrine falcon on Mount Dinham, the wings of god? Keep going... track down your own animals in shop windows, house decorations, pictures in pubs... your prey is the unnatural selection of animals that we choose.

Walk
Bites

What happened to the Bird Woman?

Mind The Gap

Begin at the cathedral, in the heart of Exeter.

Go _____ and find a place to sit for a moment.

Leave the _____ and enjoy the _____.

Find a _____ and ask for _____.

Turn _____ at the next _____ and look at the _____.

_____ for a while, before _____ the _____ sign.

Follow _____ and _____ no _____, but you can _____ with your

_____ close to _____ or _____ left _____ the _____.

_____ inside _____ several _____ here.

The _____ _____ your _____.

_____ a _____ red _____.

_____ _____ nearly _____.

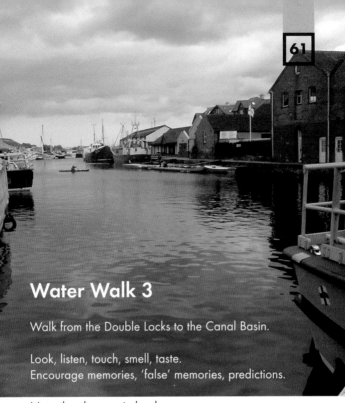

Water Walk 3

Walk from the Double Locks to the Canal Basin.

Look, listen, touch, smell, taste.
Encourage memories, 'false' memories, predictions.

Note the changes in land use:
rural
industrial
residential
leisure and heritage

Walk through the Canal Basin to Piazza Terracina.
Find somewhere to sit, looking back up the canal.

Complete the following lines:
Wherever I've lived, I've always overlooked the river...
It has a will of its own - the river...
We should have all been called fish. We loved the
water so much we should have lived in it...

Construct:
a speech to be spoken to a neighbour on the 'Southern
Comfort', as it journeys along the water from the Quay
to the Double Locks
a poem to be written along the length of the canal
in ripples
an invocation to raise the ghosts of the canal

Looking Up

Find a place where you can see good stretches of horizon. Take a deep breath and gently breathe out blowing the air along the line where everything else meets the sky. It's surprisingly relaxing.

Try the railway bridge on New North Road. Breathe out along the roofs of the Prison, the DSS building with its beautiful spiral staircase, the Exchange like a Rachel Whiteread concrete cast of the inside of somewhere else, the hills above Ide, up the spire of St Michael & All Angels on Mount Dinham and the edge of the Thistle (once Rougement) hotel on the site of the old new gaol, the trees on the volcanic knob of Northernhay Gardens, the shoulders of the Law Courts squatting on an ancient site, the Tax Building, the tip of William Kingdon Clifford's turret, the Methodist dome that took so long to build that when Sleeping Beauty awoke from her long slumber in the 1903 Theatre Royal Christmas Panto her first words to Prince Charming were: 'Have they got the roof on Sidwell Street Wesleyan Chapel yet?', the Odeon, the edges of the valley they put the railway in, the Prison again... breathe in.

from Discovering Exeter Series

Walk **B**ites — Use a mirror to view Exeter Cathedral ceiling

Memory Maps

Using only your memory, construct a map of Exeter.

Include as much detail as you can.

Walk the city according to your memory map.

And/or compare your finished map with:
a published scale map of the city
memory maps made by friends

What have you included?
What have you left out?
How do you rate your senses of scale and direction?

Walk
Bites

Ask directions to the place where you are standing

Exeter A-Z

Choose one of Exeter city centre's bus routes (labelled from 'A' to 'Z').

Buy a Stagecoach 'Day Freedom Ticket' and explore your chosen route.
Get on and off buses as you see fit.
Spend some time at the bus stops that are furthest away from the High Street.

Collect text along your route:
'found' texts - on signs, discarded pieces of paper, etc.
anecdotal evidence from members of the community - conversations with or overheard fragments spoken by people who live/work/travel on the route
personal thoughts relating to bus travel or places that you pass

Distil your material into a short text sequence.

Call Stagecoach.
Rent space for a week on the scrolling advertising signs on your chosen bus route.
Use this space to display your finished text sequence.

Or write your text on a postcard and send it to a friend who lives or works somewhere along the route.

EXETER A-Z   N   St. Davids Station - Tesco   USUALLY I GET ON THE H BUS she said   BUT TODAY I GOT ON AT THE SWIMMING BATHS   I MET MY SISTER TODAY ... radio times ... HAD A CUP OF TEA ... milk ... SHE'S NOT A BIT LIKE ME ... spaghetti x 2 (not the huge ones) ... DOESN'T AGREE WITH ANYTHING I SAY ... granulated sugar ... YOU FEEL YOU WANT TO OPEN UP TO SOMEBODY ... chicken tikka etc ... SHE DOESN'T WANT TO KNOW ... yogurt ... YOU GETTING OFF AT THIS ONE?

Repeat with other routes.

Your text(s) will help:
arouse curiosity
passengers look again at the over-familiar sites along
their journeys, framing the ordinary in an extra-ordinary
way
redress the overabundance of impersonal signage which
pervades the world

 Walk Bites

Leave a feather on the steps of Exeter Phoenix

Would you recognise Exeter by
its contours alone?

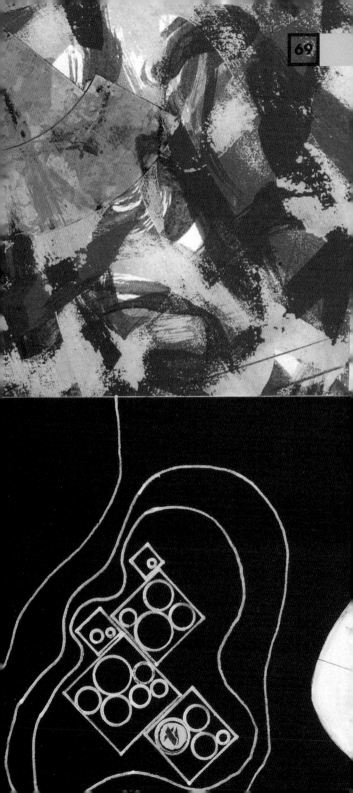

Lava flow

Take a walk guided by lava and think about how temporary the calm and stability of Exeter is. Read a history of eruption.

This is what some Exeter lava looks like:

And so is this:

The magnetic polarity of this rock – (mean directions of magnetisation of 190º declination and – 10^0 upwards inclination) - indicates that the part of the planet's skin we now call Exeter was close to the equator at the time of the volcano's eruption: the city is a site in migration, a dead volcano just passing through... As you move from rock to rock consider the liquidity of everything around you that looks so solid now.

Walk Bites

Visit the Royal Albert Museum animals whilst listening on headphones to music

cathedral - Moto - cathedral

We arranged to meet a little before daybreak at the Cathedral Close. Then set off for Southernhay, left there towards Paris Street, turned right to the roundabout, straight over and up Heavitree Road. At the Livery Dole execution site we turned right down Church Terrace – took a chance and risked a cul-de-sac – along the left hand pavement and found an alleyway. All the way down there we went, skirted the top of Sherwood Close to the church of St Michael & All Angels:

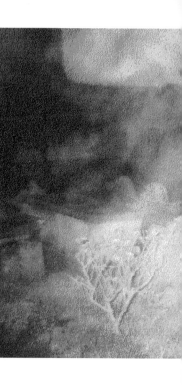

Allen Meredith looked at the tree very carefully... He came to the conclusion that what we see today is a side shoot about 4-500 years old, from a much older tree... The main tree was probably there (where the church now stands) in Saxon times.

Annabel Branney The Heavitree Yew

The yew is no ordinary tree, and is capable of renewing itself in a variety of ways, frequently for instance an aerial branch will descend down into the hollow of the trunk and root itself in the earth.

Allen Meredith A Note On The Care Of Ancient Yew Trees

Photo: Bob Butler

We found the graveyard covered in the ruins of a 'party' - ripped underwear, bottles, scooter ruts in the grass, food. And perhaps we weren't alone in being disturbed - this photograph was taken in the graveyard that morning...

Climbed over the graveyard wall into Church Street. Checked down Meadow Way for a moment. On the left - there's a plaque to an absence.

Richard Ford (1796-1858) was born in London and trained as a lawyer. In his early thirties, he moved to Spain. His journeys resulted in his Handbook for Travellers in Spain... Ford was not the first Englishman to have written about Spain, particularly the Moorish part, but 'he was the first to have explored it in such depth and to have approached its inhabitants with such sympathy'. On his return from Spain in 1834, Ford bought Heavitree House which he rebuilt in the Andalusian style... Unfortunately, a housing estate was built on the gardens in 1949, and the house itself, a rare example of the influence of Islamic art on British architecture, and the only example in the South-West, was demolished in the 1960s.

Alexander Kinglake

Backtracked up Church Street and crossing directly over Church Lane entered the hospital following the road round to the left, past the cinema-style entrance of the Orthopaedic Unit and then left down to and turned right into Bovemoor's Lane.

Turned left down Dryden Road, across Wonford Street into Coronation Road. On the left is a little passage behind the houses. Followed it to the end, trespassed through a drive, closing a gate with 'private' on it behind us, and via Willow Court picked up Coronation Road again and then straight over the roundabout on Rifford Road into Ludwell Lane. Ludd the town planner. Ludd the machine wrecker. Luddite, ludicrous, ludo. Ludd the multiple user name: Lady Ludd, Saint Leger, Lug is the British Ludd, and the Gaulish Lugd, or Lugus, patron and founder of many cities, Lug's chain (Milky Way), Lug's festival Lammas, glove, love, Hermes, Saint Michael, Moon, Monty Cantsin, Luther Blissett, A.J. Salmon, Robin Hood, Kilroy, Big Brother. About half a mile down the Lane, on the left hand side of the road and just before a farmhouse, is a rising path walled and roofed by small trees. We walked to the top with our eyes fixed on the end of the path ahead where the trees opened up to the sky and St Michael & All Angels, Heavitree 'framed in heaven.' At the stile we imagined what dreams were had on the ancient bedstead now in the brambles. (We brought a little world of wooden toy houses and left it here.) Then we turned back, left up Ludwell Lane, straight on through the industrial estate buildings, their humming ventilation, police intelligence, out onto the Rydon Lane Ring Road. Careful. Crossed it warily. Then left for a few yards and there on our right was a hole in the fence.

Careful again. Derelict houses. A stumble. A risk taken. Behind them was a delicate otherworld, the pattern of an ornamental garden grown abstract by its independence. A place to play at picnic. A place to pretend you own the house. We repaired back through the fence and right and right again into Woodwater Lane. On the left are Woodwater Cottages, peeled open as if with a tin-opener. Powdery and worn domestic satire. Carried on down the Lane. Pause. Looked back. Looked ahead. Felt the uncanny. At the end we didn't turn left with the road but carried straight on through the brambles into a temple with old mechanisms...

Minding the orchids as we came out - crossed Russell Way and onto the Grange estate, found the old psychiatric hospital buildings - in between the desirable North and South Granges are two identical and unconverted structures: his and hers mortuaries.

Out the other end of the old hospital and turned right onto the path along Baxter Close to the roundabout. Crossed and turned left up Clyst Halt Avenue for a few yards, on our right was Apple Lane Path. Took it all the way to Bishop's Court Quarry. The sandstone there was formed as 'aeolian dunes', laid down by the action of the wind; the distribution of cross-bedding azimuths in the stone indicates a prevailing wind from south-east to north-west. The quarry is a museum of breeze.

At the end of Apple Lane, turned right down Sidmouth Road, over the roundabout to Moto Services, negotiating its pedestrian-unfriendly verges. We took advantage of their 'no quibble' guarantee of 'complete satisfaction or your money back', to eat a hearty breakfast and when not 'completely satisfied' asked for our money back. Can we let the global economy palm us off with 'OK-ish' cooked breakfast as 'complete satisfaction'? As we find new ways, our ways through the city, what 'complete satisfaction' might actually be gets better and better...

Back at the cathedral we drank at the Well House and paid our respects in the cellar.

Passing Through

A meandering one mile walk, shadowing the straight line that joins Exeter's three main termini.

1: Leaving - Bus Station

Join a bus queue for a minute or two:
what place do you most treasure in Exeter?
what does the word 'leaving' mean to you?
where are the people around you going?

Leave.

2: Journeying - Bus Station to Exeter Central

Walk across Bampfylde Street and Bude Street - cut through the alleyway that leads to Debenhams - walk along New North Road and descend to a platform through the archway at the back of the station.

As you walk, think about:
your strongest memories of travelling
the direction you'd have to walk in to get home

3: Resting - Exeter Central

Find a place to sit and rest on the platform for a minute or two.

Do whatever you wish.

Walk Bites — Listen to Exeter traffic and sirens as a night at the opera

4: Journeying - Exeter Central to Exeter St Davids

Walk out onto Queen Street and head for the Clock
Tower - turn left at Exeter College, along Hele Road -
turn right down St Davids Hill - turn left at the pedestrian
crossing, and head down St Clement's Lane to
the station.

As you walk, think about:
people who might have trod this same path
things that might yet happen here

5: Arriving - Exeter St Davids

Arrive.

Stand on a platform for a minute or two:
where have the people around you come from?
what does the word 'arriving' mean to you?

Go and visit your most treasured place in Exeter

A circumambulation of Exeter Prison

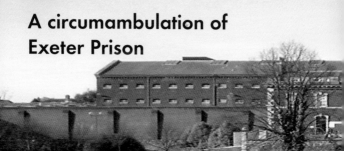

Explore the walls of the Prison, glazing it with your gaze. Along the Howell Road wall read the sentences of episodic rebuildings, bricked up gates, old wall and new wall, the 'pillars' sinking into the brick, the stone marked with the upwards arrow -

Subject: /|\ Wings of God /|\

This is taken from Mrs E. O. Gordon's book Prehistoric London - Its Mounds and Circles:

The announcement of the Divine name is the first event traditionally preserved and it occurred as follows: God, in vouchsafing His NAME said /|\ and, with the Word, all worlds and animations sprang co-instantaneously to being, and from their non-existence, shouting in ecstasy of joy /|\. Still and small was that melodious sounding voice, the primary utterance of which emanated all lays and melodies...

Use the acoustic anomaly as you pass Danes (not really) Castle on your left. Shout. Your voice escapes towards Horseguards. The wall is one to be forgotten beyond. On nights when the wind is still, disembodied voices howl hopelessly on the air - cursing and threatening each other. Beware. This is a walk in which voice and body can become separated. Think of those within. In Prison Lane - a little over halfway down young people occasionally gather to shout up to the unseen, often apparently unknown, stripteases are performed, chalking, abusive schoolkid cries of 'Are you free?' and the odd muffled reply as if from men under water growling through an overwhelming mask. What is your message?

Along the New North Road the old Police Headquarters has been swallowed into the prison, the austere façade tricked out with farcical additions busting the symmetry once proud of its orderliness. This is what 'prison reform' once looked like, built for Silent and Separate Systems: inmates respectively kept permanently in silence or in isolation. Do not speak. Be alone for a while. The building may wear a chaotic disguise now, but something still bleak and dreadful rises up from its midst in that obscene, vague tower.

And where is the fourth side? Where does it begin? Is it ever walkable? What is the fourth wall of a prison?

On the Northernhay Gardens footpaths opposite; the footfalls of ghosts, Exonians who came there to watch the hangings.

Walk Bites

Track the cats on your streets

City Planner 1

Walk along any street and re-design it to fit your desires. In your imagination you could re-organise, re-colour, re-shape the whole city. Record your new City Planning using maps, sketches, diagrams, photos. On Paris Street, imagine a new bus station or civic centre.

A good starting point could be to buy a postcard of Exeter and alter the view by sticking new images, buildings, objects onto it. An extension of this walk would be to plant some change in the street itself. For example, sticking a stamp on the pavement could mark the siting of a new post box. Where you might wish to change a colour, you leave a painting brush.

Follow the Roman Walls whilst eating a bunch of grapes

Walk Bites

City Planner 2

In 1945, just after WW2, Thomas Sharp wrote the following opening statement in 'EXETER PHOENIX: a plan for rebuilding':

The planner's first approach is to sum up the personality of the city which has been put under his care. A city has the same right as a human patient to be regarded as an individual requiring attention rather than abstract advice. That is the first thing the planner has to remind himself of. The second is that abstract principles of town planning do not in themselves produce a good plan. The good plan is that which will fulfil the struggle of the place to be itself, which satisfies what a long time ago used to be called the Genius of the Place? Has Exeter a genius?

As you wander through the city:

investigate sites that are vacant or up for redevelopment - what would you put in their place?

visit the Westcountry Studies library what has the city lost and gained over time? what plans have there been for the city that were never realised?

think about buildings, roads, districts, etc. that you could or could not do without

try to find the city's genius

Make new plans for Exeter.

Post them to the council.

Walk Bites Phone a friend describing your view from phone box or mobile

Beating The Bounds

Pick up your staff and beat out the bounds of:
the property that you live in
the old city wall
today's city of Exeter

Record significant boundary points as you move.

Explore gateways and notions of the inside(r) and the outside(r):
front doors and garden gates
old city gates (north, east, south, water and west) and breaches in the wall
major roads and waterways (if you wish to be faithful to today's city boundary you may need to pre-position cars and canoes, as it runs down the centre of the M5, the A30 and the River Exe)

Repeat annually, revisiting your chosen boundary points.

Measuring Up

Take your own body measurements.

Add a zero to each figure.

Trace the shape of a person onto a map of the city

Mark the lines and places you measured.

Walk the measurements you made, using the numbers to limit the number of paces used.

You have now mapped your body onto the city.

Did you see yourself reflected along the way?

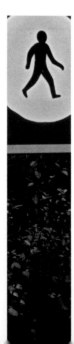

Processional Pathways

You've probably seen images of the ancient Nazca lines
- gigantic pathways in the Peruvian desert.
Sometimes geometric shapes and sometimes shaped like
animals.
They're thought to have been processional pathways.

The figures invite you to walk along them,

Dr Persis B. Clarkson.

You can create your own modern day processional
pathways on the surface of Exeter.

Get a map and a pen.
Choose a shape to walk.
Try to plot your shape on the map.

Process.

Alternatively, if you have access to a GPS device and
a computer, you can trace your path digitally by
generating a series of waypoints as you walk.
Take a look at the Global Positioning System drawing
project at www.gpsdrawing.com

Or, distort existing lines.
For example, rotate the course of the River Exe 90°,
and walk it whilst looking for connections with water.

Angry Walk

Follow an old Inuit tradition and walk
until your anger runs out. Then mark the
spot.

89

A Journey in Smell

Start outside J.L.Thomas' Animal By-products factory in Spring Gardens, by the canal. Take the path that leads under the railway to Marsh Green Road. Walk past Exeter Hide and Skin Company, Ltd. Cross Marsh Barton Road and walk past the Recycling Unit in Exton Road. Walk under the railway and up Tan Lane, into Water Lane and to the Quay. At the Quay, walk round to the boatyard and smell the paint, wood and water smells. Stop to smell the coffee in the Piazza Terracina. Head back into town, crossing Western Way and walking up West Street to Fore Street. Smell the food in the various restaurants and takeaways (kebabs, fish & chips, curry). You could pop up Bartholomew Street to the Picture House and smell the popcorn. As you head up the High Street, go into different shops, the market and the pubs and compare the smells – paper, vegetables, perfume, second hand clothes, etc. Notice the changes as you work your way up to Rougemont Gardens (on the left of the High Street, up Castle Street, next to the courts). Smell the plants and flowers here. Look out over the city.

As you go, notice any other smells you might come across.

Label and exhibit things you unearth in your back garden

Why Mis-guide?

Because we see the present flanked by memory and imagination, historical and geographical accuracy is subject to debate.
An overlay of maps seems to challenge our notions of time and space in a landscape or cityscape of sky, water and earth, merging contours, fluctuating and colliding in the flow or contra-flow of daily life.

Hence, An Exeter Mis-Guide. Hence, the strange journeys we make, walking in a place we think we know but allowing in a sense of don't know. So that we may see the windows of the houses like sky, the cracks in the pavement like rivers, the Earth in the eyes of the passers by.

Conclusion:

If you've been mis-guided enough then you'll be building up all sorts of new routes for yourself, finding your own special places and the best ways to and from them. Even your routine walks - to the shops, to work - you can be continuously refining, drawing more closely, filling with more pleasure. Don't keep the secret to yourself...

The great thing about mis-guiding is that you can use any skill or inclination that you have. As you go you can photograph, speak, memorise, video. Later you can make your own little records and pass them around. Catapults to send others on their first drift...

Selected Bibliography:

Exeter:

Discovering Exeter pamphlet series, Exeter Civic Society, Exeter: various years.

Exeter Phoenix: a plan for rebuilding, Thomas Sharp, Architectural Press for Exeter City Council, London, 1946.

The Celt and The Teuton in Exeter, Thomas Kerslake, read at the Institute, Exeter in 1873, published in The Archaeological Journal, vol. 30, 1889.

The History of the Cholera in Exeter in 1832, Thomas Shapter, John Churchill, London, 1849.

General:

City A-Z: Urban Fragments, Steve Pile and Nigel Thrift, Routledge, London, 2000.

Guidebook: three manoeuvres, Tim Brennan, Camerawords, London, 1999.

Lights Out For The Territory, Iain Sinclair, Granta Books, London, 1998.

Mutations, Rem Koolhaas, Stephano Boeri and Sandford Kwinter, ACTAR, Barcelona, 2000.

The Gentle Art of Tramping, Stephen Graham, Ernest Benn, London, 1929.

The London Adventure Or The Art of Wandering, Arthur Machen, Martin Secker, London, 1924.

The Practice Of Everyday Life Michel de Certeau, University of California Press, Berkeley, California, 1984 (1974).

Theatre/Archaeology, Mike Pearson and Michael Shanks, Routledge, London, 2001.

Walkscapes, Francesco Careri, Editorial Gustavo Gili, Barcelona, 2002.

Wanderlust, A History of Walking, Rebecca Solnit, Verso, London, 2001.

Walking in Circles, Richard Long, Thames and Hudson, London, 1991.

Webography:

Psy-Geo-Conflux:
www.glowlab.com/psygeocon/pgc_index.html

International Psychogeographic Society:
www.electricant.com/psychogeographic/magazine.htm

Exploration Station: www.explorationstation.co.uk/

Global Positioning System drawing project:
www.gpsdrawing.com/

Dread, Route and Time:
www.reconstruction.ws/home2.htm

A. J. Salmon:
www.digressmagazine.com

New York Surveillance Camera Players:
www.notbored.org/the-scp.html

Generative Psychogeography:
www.socialfiction.org/psychogeography/index.html

Met Office Weather Forecast:
www.metoffice.gov.uk/weather/europe/uk/
devoncornwall.html

Online Street Maps: www.streetmap.co.uk/

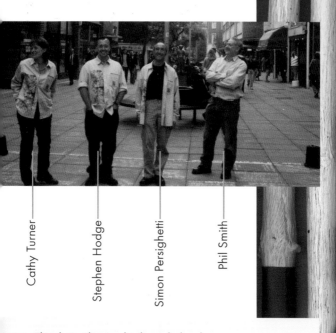

Cathy Turner

Stephen Hodge

Simon Persighetti

Phil Smith

Thanks to those who have helped us:
Sarah Bennett; David Berridge; Mary Bleasdale;
Andy Bone; Chris Burke; Bob Butler; Kevin
Cotter; Jo Cotter-Stevens; David Drake; Charlie
Fey; Matt Fletcher; Hazel Harvey; Malcolm
Haste; David Heathfield; Dee Heddon; James
Hennessy; Amy Jones; Nick Jones; Hanna
Knight; Blondel Lilley; Jo Mayes; Sian Morgan;
Anthea Nakorn; Sue Palmer; Marjorie L. Pitt;
Annette Plaut; Carolyn Purslow, Olivia &
Raphael; Pearl Putland; Maggie Squire; Claire
Stein & Ryan; Rachel Sved; Jim Thomson; Peter
Thomson; David Turner; Matthew Watkins;
Andrea Watson; Colin Whittard; David Williams;
Kay Yelland; Bong Rok, Etsuko, Haejin, Mahmut
& Mauro from Isca Language School; Available
Space; Exeter Civic Society; Exeter Forum;
Newtown Community Association; Shopmobility;
Westcountry Studies Library.

centre for creative enterprise & participation
dartington college of arts

Exeter Arts Council

Local Heritage *initiative*

Heritage Lottery Fund

Nationwide

The Countryside Agency

An Exeter Mis-Guide

An Exeter Mis-Guide is like no guide you have
ever used before. To Exeter. To Anywhere. Rather
than telling you where to go and what to see, the
Mis-Guide gives you the ways to see the Exeters
no one else has found yet. An Exeter Mis-Guide
is both a forged passport to your 'other' city and
a new way of travelling a very familiar one.
An essential part of the toolkit of any 21st Century
Exeter survivor.

THIS IS A WRIGHTS & SITES PUBLICATION

www.mis-guide.com

£4.99